# BRITAIN IN OLD

# AROUND
# WHEATLEY

*MARION GUNTHER*

ALAN SUTTON PUBLISHING LIMITED

Alan Sutton Publishing Limited
Phoenix Mill · Far Thrupp · Stroud
Gloucestershire · GL5 2BU

First published 1995

*Cover photographs: (front) a thatched cottage
in Nuneham Courtenay, late nineteenth
century; (back) the village stores, High Street,
Wheatley, c. 1930.*

**British Library Cataloguing in Publication Data.**
A catalogue record for this book is available from
the British Library.

ISBN 0-7509-0848-3

Typeset in 9/10 Sabon.
Typesetting and origination by
Alan Sutton Publishing Limited.
Printed in Great Britain by
WBC Limited, Bridgend.

For Rebecca

A panoramic view of Wheatley from Ladder Hill, *c.* 1885. The Great Western Railway station, on the Wycombe to Oxford line, is in the foreground and the church of St Mary the Virgin is in the distance.

# Contents

A Boxing Day meet of the local hunt. This traditional gathering of huntsmen and foxhounds is outside the Three Pigeons Hotel at Milton Common, near Great Milton.

# Introduction

The photographs in this book, many of which are from private collections, reveal a more tranquil way of life, and portray a variety of trades and pastimes. The largest village, aptly named Wheatley in the Valley, is six miles east of Oxford and is shielded by Shotover from the city, with hills rising steeply from all sides except the east, where the land gradually falls away to the River Thame. Roman dwellings and Saxon burial grounds have been found on both sides of Coombe Wood. At the heart of the village, High Street has pleasing seventeenth-century stone buildings on either side, and the old, much-restored manor house is at the western end. The church of St Mary the Virgin, erected in 1857, is situated in the parallel Church Road, in an elevated position above the main street. It is built of stone with a lofty tower and a broach spire containing six bells. To the west, the Round House, the village lock-up, built in 1834 and of hexagonal shape with a ball on top, is a most unusual building. A station, now gone, on the former Wycombe and Oxford section of the Great Western Railway, is an interesting feature in some of the photographs. Stones from the now disused quarries were used to build Merton College, and later produced lime; and the famous yellow ochre was quarried from the fields below the windmill. Wheatley's close proximity to Oxford has made it a popular commuter village, as attested by the new housing estates.

Horspath, the first true village east of Oxford, has attracted new housing developments, which are located on the steep hillside slopes with magnificent views of the Berkshire Downs. Older houses are grouped around The Green, with the twelfth-century church in the background. Bordering the neat green is the old Methodist Chapel, the Chequers Inn and the post office. Perhaps the most rewarding walk is along Church Road, passing the village school, the Queen's Head public house, and the old manor house. The name Horspath goes back to Anglo-Saxon times when its form was 'Horspadan', 'padan' meaning path, when pack horses used the bridleway to pass over Shotover. It is said that an Oxford student was attacked by a wild boar when walking on Shotover Hill, and escaped by ramming a volume of Aristotle down its throat; a stained glass window in St Giles's Church commemorates this. With a population of approximately two thousand inhabitants, much of the atmosphere and character of the village remain, although few people now work on the land.

Cuddesdon is situated on a high ridge approximately three miles from Wheatley and Horspath, and is approached, beyond Coombe Wood, by a minor road. The village overlooks the hamlets of Denton and Chippinghurst, and there are fine views to Brill, Wittenham Clumps and the Chilterns. The name Cuddesdon, 'hill of Cuthwine', points to an early Saxon settlement, and remains of a cemetery have been found to confirm this. From the Bishop's Palace and the Theological College the road forks at the church and descends through the main street, where there is a mixture of thatched, tiled and slate roofs. The eighteenth-century Bat and Ball Inn acquired the licence of the Three Compasses Inn, which was demolished in 1929. The road curves sharply past the old school, the village hall and the recreation ground, and descends to the attractive hamlet of Denton, where a number of old houses border The Green, fringed by a meandering stream and a bridlepath leading to Chippinghurst Manor. Denton House, bordering the road to Garsington and situated behind a large wall, dates from the early seventeenth century and has mid-eighteenth-century remodelling. Opposite the house there are seventeenth-century stables, a fifteenth/sixteenth-century barn and a large pigeon loft. The sandy soil has always been ideal for agriculture, with good pasture land near the river.

Great Milton, hidden in the valley of the Thame, remains unspoilt, with thatched cottages grouped around The Green and the Bull Inn. St Mary's Church, situated in a prominent position, is very large and light, and was built mainly in the thirteenth and fourteenth centuries. It contains the most remarkable tomb in Oxfordshire: the alabaster figures of Sir Michael Dormer (1616), his wife and father lie on a marble tomb under a gilded canopy, surrounded by other signs of earthly splendour. Near the church are two large houses: the famous, much-altered manor house, now a restaurant; and the Great House, opposite, with its elegant Georgian façade.

Toot Baldon is a small village lying away from the main roads, across the parish boundary at Baldon Brook. Attractive seventeenth-century stone cottages and the Crown public house straggle on each side of the narrow twisting lane and form the centre of the village. From the ridge there are fine views of the Chilterns across the Thame valley. The elegant Jacobean manor house and farm is situated at the north end of the parish, commanding views of Garsington and Cowley. The thirteenth-century St Lawrence's Church, slightly remote from the village and down an avenue of chestnuts, is a small building in the Transitional and Early English styles. From the church a footpath links Toot Baldon and Marsh Baldon, where a jumble of mostly sixteenth/seventeenth-century irregularly shaped, thatched, tiled and half-timbered cottages are grouped around the magnificent well-kept open green, with farms and fields beyond. This is one of the finest greens in Oxfordshire, where football, cricket and the annual fun fair are held. The village school, set back from The Green beyond a pond, has been in existence for over two hundred years. Beyond the Seven Stars public house is St Peter's Church, which is situated on slightly higher ground adjoining the seventeenth-century Baldon House. The church, shaded by trees, has an unusual octagonal bell tower with a square base, and a roughly carved sundial above the porch door, which is probably twelfth century.

Leaving the gated road from Marsh Baldon we approach the main Henley to Oxford road, and the village of Nuneham Courtenay, where there are neat rows of brick cottages with shuttered windows. At the eastern end of the road is the 'new' church of All Saints (built 1872–4), standing close to the village in a peaceful meadowland setting. The original village was pulled down in the 1760s to make way for Nuneham Park, the Harcourt mansion, and the beautiful grounds laid out by Capability Brown. The park, covering many acres, and overlooking the Thames valley, is famed for the beauty of the site, the temples, statues and follies. There is public access, from the main road, to the arboretum. The parish of Clifton Hampden is bounded on the south by the River Thames, here crossed by a substantial brick bridge of six pointed arches, dating to about 1847. St Michael and All Saints' Church is beautifully situated on a cliff overlooking the river and the centre of the village with its groups of old cottages, many of which are still thatched. The school, with its unusual clock tower, is situated opposite the post office, and newer style houses have been built on the far side of the main road. Clifton Hampden, with the Barley Mow Inn, immortalized in Jerome K. Jerome's *Three Men in a Boat*, is 'a wonderfully pretty village, old-fashioned, peaceful and dainty with flowers; the river scenery is rich and beautiful.'

The character of these villages remains relatively unchanged, although some residential development has taken place, particularly in Wheatley and Horspath. Peaceful areas are still to be found in this area of outstanding natural beauty.

*Section One*

# WHEATLEY

*Wheatley High Street.*

Ladder Hill, *c.* 1910. Looking down this steep hill across the rooftops of Wheatley, the broach spire of St Mary's Church is just visible on the right.

High Street, looking west, *c.* 1924. Once the course of a stream through the village, this road was made up in 1858. The cottage in the foreground is now tiled. Just beyond it is the post office.

High Street at the turn of the century. This view of the long, straggling High Street shows the village stores with an old motorcycle combination outside.

The Round House. This prominent landmark, an unusual hexagonal lock-up, is near the centre of the village. It was built in 1834.

The village stores, High Street, *c.* 1930. Mrs Hyde and her daughter Marjorie (who became Mrs Matthews) are in the doorway of this thriving store, which served the community of Wheatley well, before the Second World War.

Crown Road, *c.* 1897. The junction of the High Street and Friday Lane is in the distance, with the church spire beyond. The old barn in the foreground no longer exists.

The Chapel, High Street. The chapel is the central building, with Cromwell House beyond. The building on the corner in the foreground was destroyed before 1897. The identity of the one-legged gentleman, possibly an old soldier, is unknown.

Barclays Bank, High Street, 1961. This bank, reputedly the only one in England with a thatched roof, is seen here undergoing major renovation.

Wheatley schoolchildren, *c.* 1896. These Standard One pupils, in typically neat attire, are pictured with their headmaster (far right).

Children of Wheatley School at the turn of the century. The pupils are joined by Revd Maurice Bell (far left) and their headmaster (far right).

Barton Cottage, High Street. Emergency repairs are under way after it had been damaged for the fifth time. This was owing to the movement of large timber loads on their way to Baynes' Yard sawmill on Ladder Hill. The manor house is in the background.

The Crown public house, c. 1920. This coaching inn, at the east end of Wheatley, was noted for its famous stables. The archway entrance remains, but the stables have been converted into flats.

Women's Institute pageantry, *c.* 1920. This beautifully attired group is waiting its turn. Ten performances of this pageant were given.

Women's Institute pageant, *c.* 1920. The cast of the pageant, which involved the participation of all age groups, is assembled at The Windmills.

Wheatley Chapel, *c.* 1897. This auspicious occasion marked the laying of the foundation stone of the chapel schoolroom.

Wheatley schoolchildren in the late nineteenth century. They are assembled outside the school, where they fill the width of Church Road.

Celebrations for the coronation of King Edward VII, 1901. These villagers, all in their best finery, are gathered at Snow's Pit. Note the elegant dresses and hats worn by the ladies.

The blessing of the new Roman Catholic chapel at the Military Hospital, Wheatley, 17 October 1958. Those present include Archbishop D. Mathew (Roman Catholic Bishop's Officer to H.M. Forces), second from the right, and Lt. Col. A.B. Pick (Commanding Officer of the hospital), centre.

The Anglo-Saxon burial ground, *c.* 1883. The men pictured here have begun excavations.

Rectory Farm, *c.* 1920. Harvesting is under way. This was very much a family affair, with the women and children helping the menfolk with the work.

Wheatley sawmill, 3 June 1960. Mr Maurice Ashfirth, who stoked the old steam engines for fifteen years, blows the whistle for the last time. Shortly afterwards the mill was converted to electricity.

This fine traction vehicle belonged to William Avery & Sons Ltd, timber merchants of Ladder Hill. It is a wonderful example of old-fashioned working machinery.

Excavating on a yellow ochre field near Wheatley windmill, 1965. Doug Adams is on the tractor. Among other things, at one time the ochre was used for wall painting in some local churches and for painting Oxfordshire wagons. A feasibility study was carried out in 1965 to establish if any commercial use of this material could be made.

Procession to an open-air service, 1961. The rector, congregational minister and the choirboys are passing the Round House as they make their way along Church Road.

School staff, Wheatley. Those present include Revd A. Sturgess (front row, centre), Fred Sheldon, R. Leyshon, Miss J. Gast, Miss Christian and Miss L. Chapman.

Wheatley Church of England School. Situated next to the church of St Mary the Virgin, this school served the village for a great many years until its closure in 1983. Although it has now been converted to private houses, it retains the original façade.

Primary schoolchildren, 1962. These children are studying hard in the amphitheatre, situated beyond the school.

A rural science class, 1965. These boys from the third form of Wheatley Secondary School are busy working on a rotavator.

Wheatley windmills. These are the two original windmills, which were situated on the village outskirts and are recorded on Bryant's map, published in 1824. This picture is owned by Mrs Paintin, the daughter of the last working miller. The post mill, on the right, was burned down at the turn of the century.

Wheatley Mill, Mill Lane, off Ladder Hill. The octagonal shape of this eighteenth-century tower mill is unusual, since most are round. This mill is owned by Mr Len Cripps and it has been in his family for more than 120 years.

Wheatley Mill and cottage, *c*. 1930. Mr Len Cripps and his mother are at the door of their cottage, which has subsequently been enlarged and updated. The property is now occupied by Len's daughter. At this time the windmill was in a state of disrepair.

The ruined cap of the mill. The cap was damaged by lightning in 1930. A restoration society was formed in 1977 and work to restore the mill to its former glory is now being carried out.

The mill and cottage. Here the two sails, wooden-framed and rigged in canvas, are clearly visible. The first written evidence of the mill dates from 1671, when it was described as 'in a ruinous condition'.

The mill interior. This interesting view of part of the internal workings of the windmill shows the meal spout, down which the ground meal travelled.

The miller's tools. A selection of handmade tools are on the right, while on the left are seven mill bills, which were used for dressing the mill stones.

The hopper and stone case. The stone case contains a pair of mill stones. Wheatley Mill is equipped with two pairs of under-driven stones (rotated by gearing from below by a spigot drive to each pair).

Wheatley Manor, High Street, looking south-west, *c*. 1880. This is one of the oldest properties in the village and it originally overlooked the stream, at the top of the village, a favourable site where the water was at its cleanest.

Holton Water Mill, *c.* 1914. This seventeenth-century mill house lies on the banks of the River Thame on the fringe of the parish of Holton.

Holton Park, near Wheatley, *c.* 1930. This large stone building, which has a castellated parapet and other nineteenth-century Gothic features, is situated in beautiful parkland among elm and oak trees. For many years it was used as a girls' grammar school, and it is now being converted into an arts centre.

Holton Park grounds. This elegant bridge crosses the moat to an island, which can be seen from the manor house. The island is the site of a medieval dwelling, which was pulled down in about 1805.

The old stables, Holton Park. These stables are now used by Wheatley Park Comprehensive School.

The South Oxfordshire hunt, *c.* 1930. The huntsmen, horses and hounds are making their way through Holton Stone Pits, a wooded area near Wheatley.

# HORSPATH

*Camera-shy pupils of Horspath School.*

Horspath Halt. This was a station on the High Wycombe branch line from Oxford (built in 1855). It was opened in 1933 and was used by the village until 1962, when it was closed.

The Green, *c.* 1930. This view is from the post office, looking towards the railway bridge. The bridge was recently in danger of being pulled down to allow development, until residents intervened. The Chequers Inn is on the left. Behind the post office was a pound in which stray animals were kept until they were claimed.

The manor house, *c.* 1900. This is one of the most interesting buildings in the village. The house is L-shaped and built of stone, with a seventeenth-century front. It is said to be haunted.

Church Road, in the early twentieth century. The school is on the left and the manor house is on the right. The steps up to the manor house exist to this day.

The vicarage and gardens, 21 November 1980. This building is very secluded. It is situated in Church Road, with its entrance opposite the Queen's Head public house.

Horspath School, 1904. This church school for infants and juniors dates from 1738, when the incumbent paid for the education of nine poor children. In 1961 an extension was completed to cater for the rapidly growing population of Horspath.

*Top left. School interior. Large*

*classroom 1907*

*Top right. Small classroom*

*Below. School group 1909*

Horspath School interior, 1901, and pupils, 1909. The two classrooms are pictured during the time when Mr Booker was headmaster. The school group is in the playground, with the headmaster (far right) and his assistant (far left). Winifred Surman is one of the infants.

A classroom at the school, 16 July 1907. These attentive children are in the front row of a high-ceilinged classroom. They are under the instruction of Mr Booker, the headmaster. Note the wood-burning stove (centre).

An infants' class, c. 1927. At this time Miss Callard was headmistress.

Horspath schoolchildren, summer 1955. The pupils are assembled in the playground.

St Giles's Church, *c.* 1914. This church stands in the north of the village in a large churchyard. In 1849 it was 'in a dilapidated state', and work costing £800 was carried out to effect the necessary repairs.

Top left. Horspath Feast 1955
Mr. Pettigrove's roundabout has
been in the family for 62 years,
and is older than that. The legend
runs - The Pride of the South - The
Thrill of a Lifetime - Pettigrove's
Golden Galloping Horses.

Top right. Sunday School 1955
Below. The Feast

Horspath Feast and Sunday School, 1955. The traditional fair is still held annually on The Green. The Sunday School group is pictured outside St Giles's Church.

A local couple, in the late nineteenth century. Mr Harris was shepherd to Mr A. Walker, a farmer.

Littleworth brickworks from the railway line, c. 1930. The line closed in 1962, and no longer exists. An industrial estate has replaced the brickworks.

Littleworth village from the railway bridge, c. 1908. The land in the foreground is now occupied by light industrial units.

# CUDDESDON

*Potato pickers at Blay's Farm.*

High Street, *c.* 1910. The school, no longer in use, is on the near right and the eighteenth-century Bat and Ball Inn is beyond it.

A peaceful scene, looking towards All Saints' Church, May 1908. Groups of cottages, some thatched, form a picturesque view of the main street.

All Saints' Church, *c.* 1906. Note the lychgate and the prominent central tower.

The church and graveyard, *c.* 1940.
This view is from the lychgate.

High Street in the late nineteenth century, before the road was made up. The Three
Compasses Inn on the left no longer exists, having been destroyed in the mid-1920s.
The large tree in the distance stood at the fork of the roads to Wheatley and to Milton.

Mr A. Foster standing in the doorway of his solid stone house, High Street.

Cuddesdon Football Team, outside the pavilion in College Field, *c.* 1950. Robert 'Bob' Runcie, the then Rector of Cuddesdon and principal of Cuddesdon College (now Ripon College), is on the far left of the back row. He later became Archbishop of Canterbury (1980–91). Among the village men is Michael Sawyer, who is third from left in the back row.

Cuddesdon Football Team, outside Cuddesdon village hall, 1934. Harry Sawyer is in the centre of the back row.

Cuddesdon Football Team, cup winners, 1954. The team is pictured with the coveted trophy. Most villages had a football team as there were usually enough young men with sufficient interest in the game.

Woodworking class, c. 1890. These boys are learning a trade from their woodwork master. The photograph was taken by Joseph Turrill.

Guides and Brownies, early 1940s. Betty Foster is on the far right of the front row.

Potato picking, Blay's Farm, *c*. 1940. Joe Foster is driving the tractor.

John Sawyer sweeping the snow. Mr Sawyer, pictured here at the age of eighty-four, is in the grounds of Cuddesdon College, where he worked. After retiring he lived to the great age of one hundred at 27 High Street, where he died. The Sawyers are the oldest established family in the village.

Harry Sawyer near Cuddesdon Mill, early 1950s. He is displaying a fine catch after fishing in the River Thame, at a time when this was a favourite pastime for village men.

Coal merchant Harry Sawyer in the garden of his home, holding his baby son, Michael.

Grandpa John Sawyer. He is pictured with his 4½-month-old grandson on his knee in the vegetable garden of his home.

Wedding group, All Saints' Church, 9 June 1923. Emily Foster, the bride, and her attendants are carrying simple bouquets of moon daisies.

The happy couple, Emily and Joe Foster.

Arthur Joseph Foster, First World War. Mr Foster was a member of the Oxfordshire Yeomanry.

Fourth Oxfordshire Home Guard, Cuddesdon, Second World War. Joe Foster is at the far right of the front row.

Mr and Mrs Evans, a hard-working couple, are taking a break.

Joe Foster, 'Dad', Blay's Farm, *c.* 1940. He is working on this wide sweep of meadowland with a good view beyond.

Wedding group, Cuddesdon village hall, 15 May 1949. The bride, Marlene, is seated on the far left, with members of the Sawyer family. From left to right: Bob, Grace, Harry, 'Grampa' John, Arthur and Lou.

Betty Foster and Revd Mr Joyce, *c*. 1940. This charming photograph was taken in the cricket field.

Cuddesdon Palace, *c.* 1890. This view shows the drive and front entrance of the palace, which is the residence of the Bishop of Oxford. The original palace, built between 1632 and 1641, was destroyed in the Civil War. Bishop Bancroft was the first Bishop of Oxford to reside at Cuddesdon.

Miss Ivy Sawyer, *c.* 1920. Ivy is standing in the vegetable garden at 27 High Street. Home-grown vegetables were the mainstay of the diet in those days.

Betty Foster. Aged eighteen months, Betty was in her best velvet dress, no doubt for a special occasion.

Mr Harry Sawyer taking a break after a busy day in the garden, Mill House, *c.* 1930. He lived at the mill and worked for twenty-three years as gardener.

Cuddesdon Mill. The horse is patiently waiting for the cart to be unloaded. The road leads back to the village, approximately one mile away.

This picture was taken from the corner of the mill and shows the narrow, twisting road and the two bridges, with their elegant stone arches, spanning the mill stream and the River Thame, c. 1920.

Harry Sawyer at the mill, *c*. 1920. Mr Sawyer is sitting on the filter gate beneath the bridge. His nephew is on the far right.

Denton House. This house, with its enclosed gardens with daffodils carpeting the lawn, dates from the sixteenth century.

Ruins in the grounds of Denton House. The boundary wall to the garden contains fragments of late medieval tracery. The original east window from Brasenose Chapel, Oxford, is the main feature shown.

A bathing place in the grounds of Chippinghurst Manor gardens, created from a backwater of the River Thame. The river follows the line of trees in the background.

A solid row of houses in High Street, at the turn of the century. The Bat and Ball Inn is in the distance. These properties still stand.

Harry Sawyer and his brother, at the gate near Cuddesdon Mill, *c.* 1920.

# GREAT MILTON

*Gypsy folk on local farmland.*

Lower End, *c.* 1920. This unhurried, tranquil scene is typical of the period.

Row of thatched cottages, looking on to The Green. The Bull Inn is nearby. The character of this area remains today.

Row of cottages, The Green. These buildings remain unchanged.

Great Milton House, *c.* 1920. The structure of this house is much the same today. St Mary's Church is in the background.

St Mary's Church, from the north-east, *c.* 1870. A fine example of dry stone walling can be seen in the foreground.

St Mary's Church. The old manor gates are clearly visible in the wall on the left. Oliver Cromwell is said to have passed through these gates on his way from the Battle of Chalgrove Field to Thame.

Great Milton Priory, 1901. This photograph was taken across the meadows from the west. A pretty thatched cottage is visible on the left.

Interior of Great Milton Priory, 1943. This room on the ground floor has fine wooden panelling and an impressive fireplace.

A village outing, *c.* 1923. The party is in an open-topped charabanc fitted with solid tyres. The old village saddler, Mr Burroughs, is one of the happy throng.

A charabanc outing, 2 May 1932.

Mount Pleasant, Thame Road. This was the home of the Smith family. The large yew tree has a seat carved in it, facing the front door, to provide a cool summer retreat.

'Old man Smith', in the early twentieth century. Mr Smith farmed at Mount Pleasant.

William Smith, *c.* 1930. He was also a farmer.

Miss Nellie Smith and her dog. Nellie was a schoolmistress at Great Milton for forty years.

The Smith family, outside Mount Pleasant. Mr and Mrs Smith are pictured with their children, Nellie, Lilian, Albert, Fred and Harold, and the family dog.

A charming portrait of Miss M.A. Nudge aged two years and nine months, Christmas 1934. She is a relative of the Smith family.

The Smith family, outside the entrance to Mount Pleasant. Lilian and Nellie Smith are receiving their guests for a christening. They have arrived in a Wolseley – a proud possession no doubt.

Mothers' Union outing, *c.* 1925. Village women and their children are enjoying a trip on the River Thames, which was organized by Mrs Potts.

This view across the meadowland is looking towards the centre of the village, with horses in the foreground, *c.* 1930.

Miss Ella Constable and her companions, at the turn of the century.

Silver Jubilee celebrations, 1935. The row of banners were erected to commemorate the jubilee of George V. They are pictured outside the gates of Monkery Farm, with a group of villagers ready for celebrations in the barn.

A party in the dining hall of Milton House. This party was given by Mr Lawrence, then a housemaster of Eton College.

Steam threshing on the Smith family farm, Mount Pleasant, *c.* 1920. This was a dusty, dirty job for the farmhands.

Great Milton Football Team, 1922. This was a winning side, as can be seen from the trophies. Mr Albert Matthews is believed to be on the far right of the front row.

Bellringers' trip, c. 1920. Mr Percival Potts, then Lord of the Manor, organized outings for the village ringers each year.

Comrades' reunion. This cheerful gathering of old soldiers includes Mr Fred Smith, who is sitting next to the bemedalled pensioner.

Second World War veterans enjoying a social evening, *c.* 1950. Mr Reg Payne is sitting at the far right.

Army group, *c.* 1932. Great Milton men Fred Smith and Reg Payne (front right) are among the comrades taking time off to relax.

Mr Roy Sawyer, Second World War. Mr Sawyer, of Great Milton, is in service under canvas.

This violin player is entertaining a happy group of gypsies on local farmland, *c*. 1920. Note the beautiful horse-drawn caravan in the background.

Schoolchildren in fancy dress, 1935. These children are dressed up for a Christmas play.

Great Milton schoolchildren. This solemn class is pictured with its teacher, Miss Nellie Smith. The surnames of two of the boys are Booker and Hayes.

School gardening group, 1915. These village boys with their teacher are pictured on school land. They are learning the art of vegetable-growing, hence the large garden tools.

Schoolchildren in the playground, *c.* 1915. These children are from a primary class.

Infant class, 1929. The children's teacher is Miss Nellie Smith. The picture was taken in the playground, by the school door.

Junior class, 1958. These pupils are pictured in the playground with their teacher.

Miss Lilian Smith and a friend, outside the Cromwell Gates, *c.* 1920.

Thatched cottage. This pretty, well-kept cottage enjoys a prominent position on The Green.

Schoolchildren in costume, *c.* 1936. These children are pictured just before judging in the fancy dress competition, which was an important part of the village pageant.

Maypole dancing, early twentieth century. These children in their beautiful clothes and pictured with their teachers, are thought to be in the grounds of the manor house.

Prize chrysanthemums, *c.* 1930. This proud local couple are pictured with their best blooms.

Great Milton playing field. Jack Allen, a churchwarden and newsagent before and during the Second World War, is officiating at the opening ceremony of the play area. The children are eagerly awaiting their turn on the slide.

Harrowing, mid-1920s. Mr Harold Smith, for some obscure reason known as the 'farm drudge', is in charge of this pair of fine horses.

Miss Lilian Smith, c. 1920. Lilian, a farmer's daughter, is on the traction engine. She is reputed to have worked very hard on the family farm.

Mr Fred Smith with First World War comrades, enjoying a pint and a chat.

*Section Five*

# THE BALDONS

*Members of the Women's Institute, some from Toot
Baldon, enjoying a charabanc trip.*

The Crown public house, *c.* 1899. This seventeenth-century inn is situated on the main road in the centre of the village. At one time Mr Pitson was the landlord.

Manor House, *c.* 1944. This three-storeyed stone house, with a roof of unusual tiles and huge brick chimneys, is enclosed within a walled garden opposite Court House.

St Lawrence's Church, from the south-west, *c.* 1880. This fine example of a small, thirteenth-century building is oblong in plan with a chancel and nave of the same width.

St Lawrence's Church. This is the north doorway, which has a fine stone arch. This entrance is now rarely used.

The Crown public house, *c.* 1910. This stone building remains much the same today. Greystone Cottage and Willoughby Cottage are in the background; both of them now have tiled roofs. A splendid horse chestnut tree towers over the roof of the public house.

Toot Baldon Mother's Union outing at the turn of the century. Among the passengers are members of the Druce and Clinkard families.

Members of the Women's Institute, some from Toot Baldon, are arriving at Maidenhead in a charabanc for a pleasant day out.

Herbert and Florrie Barrett outside their cottage, *c.* 1930. The Barretts lived at no. 17 Toot Baldon. Mr Barrett was a threshing-machine driver.

A Toot Baldon family, *c.* 1920. Mr and Mrs Jack Druce are pictured with their son William and daughter Nancy outside their home, after they had moved to Nuneham Courtenay. Note the old shuttered windows.

Florrie Barrett with her grandson, G. Druce, *c.* 1939. They are pictured under the large chestnut trees at the entrance to the church avenue.

Family outing, *c.* 1900. These village families are about to leave on a day trip in an old motorcoach. All are well prepared for inclement weather! The names of those present include Druce and Pitson. Mr David Clinkard is in the centre of the picture.

Greystone Cottage, *c.* 1910. This building, situated near the Crown public house, now has a tiled roof.

Willoughby Cottage. This large, thatched cottage was built in 1774. The roof has now been tiled. At one time the Abel and Barrett families lived here. The people in the front garden, where roses ramble up to the eaves of the house, may be from these families.

Threshing by the barn, *c*. 1910. This was a common sight on the farms in bygone days. Mr Herbert Barrett can be seen in the background, feeding the sheaves into the drum.

Wedding group, *c.* 1930. This picture was taken behind the Crown public house on the occasion of Annie Pitson's wedding to Arthur Higgins. Those present include all of the Pitson sisters. Eventually the couple took over the running of the Crown public house.

Mr and Mrs Jack Druce and their son William. The family is pictured in the garden of Fern Cottage, Garsington, home of the photographer Joseph Turrill.

Two of the Pitson sisters in their finery and lace. The sisters lived at the Crown public house.

Toot Baldon schoolchildren, *c*. 1927.

Villagers outside the barn in the late nineteenth century.

Pupils of Toot Baldon Church School, *c.* 1906. Their teachers, Mr and Mrs Lewis, are present, and among the pupils are members of the Barrett and Pitson families.

The Home Guard on parade during the Second World War. Toot Baldon and Marsh Baldon men are marching down the main street in the neighbouring village of Nuneham Courtenay.

St Peter's Church, June 1906. This view is from the south-east, and shows the fourteenth-century west tower and the graveyard.

The tower of St Peter's Church. This unusual tower has a solid square base and an octagonal top, which may have been built to support a steeple. In the background is Baldon House.

Sundial over the south door of the church. This doorway has a scratch dial with a cabled border and is the only piece of Saxon work remaining in the church. It is listed as one of the twenty-four certain Anglo-Saxon sundials known in the country.

This beautiful picture by Henry Taunt shows the village pond in springtime, *c.* 1900. The school is just beyond it with pretty cottages grouped around.

The ancient tree. This tree has for centuries been a landmark on Marsh Baldon Green, until recently when the hollowed shell of the trunk, which was all that remained, had to be removed for safety reasons.

The Green, *c.* 1920. Many of these thatched and tiled cottages remain to this day.

Sarah Gooding by the wishing well on The Green in the late nineteenth century. When this photograph was taken, Sarah was one hundred years old.

Pupils of Marsh Baldon School at the turn of the century. The entire school is present; all are well wrapped up against the cold with large fur hats and trimmed coats.

Marsh Baldon House, *c.* 1890. This elegant seventeenth-century brick building is covered with rough-cast and has a roof of old red tiles. Three pinnacled gables adorn the front of the house. This photograph was taken by Joseph Turrill.

# NUNEHAM COURTENAY & CLIFTON HAMPDEN

*A tranquil scene by the River Thames, Clifton Hampden.*

General store and post office, *c.* 1920. The main street of Nuneham Courtenay is now a very busy road. Two rows of identical, neat eighteenth-century cottages with shuttered windows border each side of the street. This was known as the 'New Town': the original village was alongside the River Thames inside Nuneham Park.

Road improvements, March 1959. Road widening and relevelling is under way on the outskirts of the village to cope with increased traffic. The dense woods are characteristic of this area.

All Saints' Church from the south-east, *c.* 1880. This eighteenth-century church is a well-proportioned building of freestone and is set in idyllic surroundings of meadowland.

The Harcourt Arms Hotel, *c.* 1930. This building is situated at the east end of the village and is an attractive U-shaped structure with eighteenth-century details. Note the beautiful horse chestnut tree in full bloom.

The main street, looking north, *c*. 1907. This shows a good view of the neat rows of two-storey cottages, built of chequered brick of a warm rose colour and bordered by wide grass verges.

Cuckham Lodge, *c.* 1906. This somewhat grand entrance to Nuneham Park, flanked by high trees, is seen from inside the grounds of the park.

The main façade of Nuneham Courtenay House, c. 1906. This impressive building is situated within a considerable wooded area, which extends down to the River Thames.

Nuneham Park, c. 1882. This view of an elegant bridge is from the Oxfordshire bank of the River Thames and shows some of the park's extensive woodland.

The River Thames, Nuneham Park, *c.* 1882. Groups of people are enjoying a fête day –
chatting, picnicking and boating on a beautiful summer's day.

A beautiful picture of a thatched cottage, late nineteenth century. It is situated in Nuneham Park on the bank of the River Thames. Sitting on the grass, beneath a rose archway, some young girls are posing in their best dresses. On the water are swans and cygnets.

St Michael's Church and village shop, *c.* 1930. The church is situated in the centre of the village, and dwarfs the shop. The shop now has a tiled roof, but the three large, ornate chimneys remain.

A well-kept thatched cottage, *c.* 1930. This a typical example of dwellings in this charming village, many of which still stand.

Clifton Hampden School and schoolhouse, *c.* 1880. The unusual square tower carries a bell and clock on two faces, with the main classroom extending on either side. An additional single-storey classroom has since been built in the foreground.

The village from the steep steps of St Michael's Church. In the background, behind the group of thatched cottages, is the school. The roof in the foreground, which belongs to the village shop, is now tiled.

A stone and tiled cottage with an adjoining, thickly thatched dwelling, in the centre of the village, *c.* 1900.

The Barley Mow Inn, *c.* 1877. This famous inn, immortalized in *Three Men in a Boat*, is pictured before any extensions (see p. 125) and subsequent damage due to fire. This inn was built in 1352.

St Michael's Church, *c.* 1909. Looking from the north, the post office/shop can be seen in the foreground. From the porch of the church there are magnificent views of the River Thames and the road bridge.

The manor house, *c.* 1930. This stately building is set in beautiful gardens with imposing views of the Chilterns. The house has an interesting, open bell tower, topped by a weather-vane and, apart from the addition of an extension, is little changed to this day.

This panoramic view of the River Thames, framed by trees and with the wooded countryside beyond, shows the bridge with its six elegant, pointed arches.

The opening of the new Scout hut, *c.* 1980. Leaders Bill Oldroyd and Peter Phillips, together with a group of Scouts, proudly display their banner. This Scout group was formed in 1961, followed by the Cubs in 1964. They met in the village hall until the opening of their own hut on the playing field.

Pleasure steamer on the River Thames, 1962. The prominent tower of St Michael's Church is in the background.

The bridge over the River Thames, *c.* 1887. This view is from the south bank. The bridge was built as a replacement for the original ferry.

This wide stretch of the river is just below the village and has a riverside footpath.

The toll bridge and keeper's house, 1930. Traffic lights are now in place on each side of this single-carriageway bridge over the River Thames.

Clifton Lock, *c.* 1950. This lock, built in 1822, is to be found half a mile upstream from Clifton Hampden bridge in its own side-stream off the main course of the River Thames. The current lock-keeper, Peter Rowe, who has served there for twelve years, is also a village bell-ringer and a wood carver of some repute.

The Barley Mow Inn on the River Thames, at the turn of the century. Behind the inn a rather austere annexe is visible. This has now been replaced by a thatched extension, in keeping with the main building, which retains much of its beamed and thatched structure.

# Acknowledgements

I would like to thank the many people who have helped me to compile this book. First, may I thank Mr Peter Gidney and Mr Mark Gunther for checking, correcting and typing; Nuala la Vertue, Oxfordshire Photographic Archive, for giving me access to the photographs, and for her general help and patience; Dr Malcolm Graham, Head of Oxfordshire Studies, for checking the text. I am especially grateful to the following people who lent me photographs and told me fascinating stories to go with them: Mrs Claydon, Mr L. Cripps, Mrs G. Druce, Mr R. Mathews, Mr A. Parker, Mrs Phipps and Mr H. Sawyer. Without them this book would not have been possible.

# Sources

Bloxham, Christine, *Portrait of Oxfordshire*.
Rimmer, Alfred, *Pleasant Spots around Oxford*.
Lethbridge, Richard, *Oxfordshire and Berkshire*, *New Shell Guides*.
*St Giles, Horspath*: Church Guide.
Jerome, Jerome K., *Three Men in a Boat*.
*The Victoria History of the County of Oxford*, vol. 5, Bullingdon Hundred.
Oxfordshire Record Society: Wheatley Records 956–1956.
Oxfordshire County Council Leisure and Arts, Central Library, Westgate, Oxford.

The author/compiler accepts no responsibility for any errors or inaccuracies in the captions, which are based on people's memories.

# BRITAIN IN OLD PHOTOGRAPHS

To order any of these titles please telephone Littlehampton Book Services on 01903 721596

## ALDERNEY

Alderney: A Second Selection, *B Bonnard*

## BEDFORDSHIRE

Bedfordshire at Work, *N Lutt*

## BERKSHIRE

Maidenhead, *M Hayles & D Hedges*
Around Maidenhead, *M Hayles & B Hedges*
Reading, *P Southerton*
Reading: A Second Selection, *P Southerton*
Sandhurst and Crowthorne, *K Dancy*
Around Slough, *J Hunter & K Hunter*
Around Thatcham, *P Allen*
Around Windsor, *B Hedges*

## BUCKINGHAMSHIRE

Buckingham and District, *R Cook*
High Wycombe, *R Goodearl*
Around Stony Stratford, *A Lambert*

## CHESHIRE

Cheshire Railways, *M Hitches*
Chester, *S Nichols*

## CLWYD

Clwyd Railways, *M Hitches*

## CLYDESDALE

Clydesdale, *Lesmahagow Parish Historical Association*

## CORNWALL

Cornish Coast, *T Bowden*
Falmouth, *P Gilson*
Lower Fal, *P Gilson*
Around Padstow, *M McCarthy*
Around Penzance, *J Holmes*
Penzance and Newlyn, *J Holmes*
Around Truro, *A Lyne*
Upper Fal, *P Gilson*

## CUMBERLAND

Cockermouth and District, *J Bernard Bradbury*
Keswick and the Central Lakes, *J Marsh*
Around Penrith, *F Boyd*
Around Whitehaven, *H Fancy*

## DERBYSHIRE

Derby, *D Buxton*
Around Matlock, *D Barton*

## DEVON

Colyton and Seaton, *T Gosling*
Dawlish and Teignmouth, *G Gosling*
Devon Aerodromes, *K Saunders*
Exeter, *P Thomas*
Exmouth and Budleigh Salterton, *T Gosling*
From Haldon to Mid-Dartmoor, *T Hall*
Honiton and the Otter Valley, *J Yallop*
Around Kingsbridge, *K Tanner*
Around Seaton and Sidmouth, *T Gosling*
Seaton, Axminster and Lyme Regis, *T Gosling*

## DORSET

Around Blandford Forum, *B Cox*
Bournemouth, *M Colman*
Bridport and the Bride Valley, *J Burrell & S Humphries*
Dorchester, *T Gosling*
Around Gillingham, *P Crocker*

## DURHAM

Darlington, *G Flynn*
Darlington: A Second Selection, *G Flynn*
Durham People, *M Richardson*
Houghton-le-Spring and Hetton-le-Hole, *K Richardson*
Houghton-le-Spring and Hetton-le-Hole:
    A Second Selection, *K Richardson*
Sunderland, *S Miller & B Bell*
Teesdale, *D Coggins*
Teesdale: A Second Selection, *P Raine*
Weardale, *J Crosby*
Weardale: A Second Selection, *J Crosby*

## DYFED

Aberystwyth and North Ceredigion,
    *Dyfed Cultural Services Dept*
Haverfordwest, *Dyfed Cultural Services Dept*
Upper Tywi Valley, *Dyfed Cultural Services Dept*

## ESSEX

Around Grays, *B Evans*

## GLOUCESTERSHIRE

Along the Avon from Stratford to Tewkesbury, *J Jeremiah*
Cheltenham: A Second Selection, *R Whiting*
Cheltenham at War, *P Gill*
Cirencester, *J Welsford*
Around Cirencester, *E Cuss & P Griffiths*
Forest, The, *D Mullin*
Gloucester, *J Voyce*
Around Gloucester, *A Sutton*
Gloucester: From the Walwin Collection, *J Voyce*
North Cotswolds, *D Viner*
Severn Vale, *A Sutton*
Stonehouse to Painswick, *A Sutton*
Stroud and the Five Valleys, *S Gardiner & L Padin*
Stroud and the Five Valleys: A Second Selection,
    *S Gardiner & L Padin*
Stroud's Golden Valley, *S Gardiner & L Padin*
Stroudwater and Thames & Severn Canals,
    *E Cuss & S Gardiner*
Stroudwater and Thames & Severn Canals: A Second
    Selection, *E Cuss & S Gardiner*
Tewkesbury and the Vale of Gloucester, *C Hilton*
Thornbury to Berkeley, *J Hudson*
Uley, Dursley and Cam, *A Sutton*
Wotton-under-Edge to Chipping Sodbury, *A Sutton*

## GWYNEDD

Anglesey, *M Hitches*
Gwynedd Railways, *M Hitches*
Around Llandudno, *M Hitches*
Vale of Conwy, *M Hitches*

## HAMPSHIRE

Gosport, *J Sadden*
Portsmouth, *P Rogers & D Francis*

## HEREFORDSHIRE

Herefordshire, *A Sandford*

## HERTFORDSHIRE

Barnet, *I Norrie*
Hitchin, *A Fleck*
St Albans, *S Mullins*
Stevenage, *M Appleton*

## ISLE OF MAN

The Tourist Trophy, *B Snelling*

## ISLE OF WIGHT

Newport, *D Parr*
Around Ryde, *D Parr*

## JERSEY

Jersey: A Third Selection, *R Lemprière*

## KENT

Bexley, *M Scott*
Broadstairs and St Peter's, *J Whyman*
Bromley, Keston and Hayes, *M Scott*
Canterbury: A Second Selection, *D Butler*
Chatham and Gillingham, *P MacDougall*
Chatham Dockyard, *P MacDougall*
Deal, *J Broady*
Early Broadstairs and St Peter's, *B Wootton*
East Kent at War, *D Collyer*
Eltham, *J Kennett*
Folkestone: A Second Selection, *A Taylor & E Rooney*
Goudhurst to Tenterden, *A Guilmant*
Gravesend, *R Hiscock*
Around Gravesham, *R Hiscock & D Grierson*
Herne Bay, *J Hawkins*
Lympne Airport, *D Collyer*
Maidstone, *I Hales*
Margate, *R Clements*
RAF Hawkinge, *R Humphreys*
RAF Manston, *RAF Manston History Club*
RAF Manston: A Second Selection,
    *RAF Manston History Club*
Ramsgate and Thanet Life, *D Perkins*
Romney Marsh, *E Carpenter*
Sandwich, *C Wanostrocht*
Around Tonbridge, *C Bell*
Tunbridge Wells, *M Rowlands & I Beavis*
Tunbridge Wells: A Second Selection,
    *M Rowlands & I Beavis*
Around Whitstable, *C Court*
Wingham, Adisham and Littlebourne, *M Crane*

## LANCASHIRE

Around Barrow-in-Furness, *J Garbutt & J Marsh*
Blackpool, *C Rothwell*
Bury, *J Hudson*
Chorley and District, *J Smith*
Fleetwood, *C Rothwell*
Heywood, *J Hudson*
Around Kirkham, *C Rothwell*
Lancashire North of the Sands, *J Garbutt & J Marsh*
Around Lancaster, *S Ashworth*
Lytham St Anne's, *C Rothwell*
North Fylde, *C Rothwell*
Radcliffe, *J Hudson*
Rossendale, *B Moore & N Dunnachie*

## LEICESTERSHIRE

Around Ashby-de-la-Zouch, *K Hillier*
Charnwood Forest, *I Keil, W Humphrey & D Wix*
Leicester, *D Burton*
Leicester: A Second Selection, *D Burton*
Melton Mowbray, *T Hickman*
Around Melton Mowbray, *T Hickman*
River Soar, *D Wix, P Shacklock & I Keil*
Rutland, *T Clough*
Vale of Belvoir, *T Hickman*
Around the Welland Valley, *S Mastoris*

## LINCOLNSHIRE

Grimsby, *J Tierney*
Around Grimsby, *J Tierney*
Grimsby Docks, *J Tierney*
Lincoln, *D Cuppleditch*